TREASURES FROM MY HEART

THE ART OF NAVIGATING LIFE WITH THE WORD

JEANETTE MCCARTHY

Flow DIVINE
PUBLISHING

CONTENTS

All Hebraic translations have been taken from Biblehub.com or The Complete Word Study Old Testament Word Study Series.

Jeanette McCarthy/Divine Flow Publishing

71-75 Shelton Street, Covent Garden,

London, WC2H 9JQ, United Kingdom

www.jeanettemccarthy.com

Book Cover © 2021 Chrispel Media

Treasures From My Heart/ Jeanette McCarthy.

ISBN 978-1-8383685-0-0

The power to change your life is in reading, studying and speaking God's word out loud.
Jeanette McCarthy

Death and life are in the power of the tongue,
And those who love it will eat its fruit.
Proverbs 18:21

Study this Book of Instruction continually. Meditate on it day and night so you will be sure to obey everything written in it. Only then will you prosper and succeed in all you do.
Joshua 1:8

∽

Hebraic translations have been taken from Biblehub.com or 'The Complete Word Study Old Testament Word Study Series.'

This book is dedicated to my Mum and Dad and all those who seek to walk worthy of God who called them into His Kingdom.

Luke 6:45 (NLT)
"A good person produces good things from the treasury of a good heart, and an evil person produces evil things from the treasury of an evil heart. What you say flows from what is in your heart."

Matthew 13:52 (NKJV)
"Then He said to them, "Therefore every scribe instructed concerning the kingdom of heaven is like a householder who brings out of his treasure things new and old."

ACKNOWLEDGMENTS

I want to thank my Lord and Saviour Jesus Christ. You are the reason I live. Thank you for being so patient with me and walking with me day by day. Your truths are the treasures of my heart, that are lighting my way and showing me how to navigate through life.

Thank you to Jaki Carty, your passion and love for the Bible inspires me to know His Word more. Thank you for your exceptional proofreading skills and being a great sounding board. Your insights were invaluable. Love you my sister in Christ.

Thank you to Camelle Daley, book coach and marketing extra-ordinaire. Thank you for championing my work, for your prayers and your tireless work to get this book to print. Working with you is always an absolute joy. Love you always my dear friend and sister in Christ.

Thank you to Co-Pastor Marie, my very dear friend, mentor, and sister in Christ. Thank you for using your phenomenal designing talents to make my book look AMAZING! Your creative gifts are exceptional, and your support and encouragement is one of the reasons why I'm a writer and why this book exists.

Letter To Reader

Dear Reader, you are very precious to God and deeply loved. Wherever you are in your faith journey and in your walk with the Lord, know that God is for you.

Let God help you and teach you more about Himself and who you are in Christ.

God delights to see your growth and progress in Him. Each step of faith you take you are becoming more like Jesus. God's plans for you are good and full of hope. There is no part of your life and nothing that you go through that God wants you to face alone.

Bring all that you are to Him. The good and the bad, your struggles and your weaknesses. You don't have to live under a cloud of guilt and condemnation. Let God show you through His Word how to navigate every season of your life, so you can know for yourself, God's good, acceptable and perfect plan, and purpose for your life.

INTRODUCTION

It was my aim to publish this book on my birthday which was on 27th January. But as the day drew closer, I felt an impression from God that now was not the time.

I decided to do all the prep work ready for publication just in case I had misheard, but suddenly little things started to not go to plan, and it became clear the book would not be ready for publication. I was a little disappointed and I wasn't sure of the reason for the delay? But it wouldn't be long before I found out.

Literally overnight I found myself in a season of intense spiritual heart surgery. God was dealing with my heart and it was painful.

I felt like my senses were heightened to the sin in my heart. I felt awful, was I really such a terrible person? Then I caught COVID. The first five days were the worst, I had migraines, my body ached and I had serious fatigue. One night as I tossed and turned in pain in bed, I suddenly felt the presence of the Holy

Spirit. He came to me as the Teacher and He gave me 1 Peter 5:10. I remembered the verse but grabbed my bible to read it.

1 Peter 5:10 NKJV

But may the God of all grace, who called us to His eternal glory by Christ Jesus, after you have suffered a while, perfect, establish, strengthen, and settle you.

As I lay on my bed praising God through my pain, my heart filled with hope that Jesus was with me. Since that night, I have been holding onto this promise as God works on my heart. As the weeks went on God led me to various scriptures. Psalms 119, James 4, Jeremiah 29:13, 1 John 4:16, Hebrews 4:16 and Galatians 3: 1-7.

Then He began to deal with me about prayer and spending time in His word.

It's been a journey but like **Psalm 119:71** says.

It is good for me that I have been afflicted,
That I may learn Your statutes.

As I was sharing this season in my life with a friend, she told me *"...these seasons never really end. Those of us who desire to walk with God will be continually pruned by Him..."* Interestingly in our church Bible study we were studying St John chapter 15 where Jesus teaches us about abiding and pruning. We know that our Heavenly Father leads us through this process so we can bear more fruit in our lives.

Sometimes the greatest treasures God has for us come out of the most painful times. We don't have to fear these seasons, because the love of God keeps us. God knows how to take care of His own, He knows the path we take, and when He has tested us we will come out as refined gold. (Job 23:10).

CHAPTER ONE: GENESIS

CREATION

Genesis 1:1 (NKJV)

In the beginning God created the heavens and the earth.

THOUGHT

*H*ere is where we first meet God. He tells us right from the start He exists, and He was at the beginning. When someone gets ready to tell you a story or give an account, and they say to you, *I was there from the start,* you put more stock in what they have to say. They are not like the person who only came in halfway through and gave you a partial account. No, God has the best perspective because He saw how everything unfolded from the beginning.

The next thing God tells us is He created the Heavens and the Earth. So, not only is He the owner of everything, but He is supremely powerful, highly intelligent, an artist, an inventor, an architect, a designer with the imagination, vision, and ingenuity of…well…God. Not a god, but THE God.

When we understand and accept that we have a creator and everything around us we can see was created by Him (be it nature, stars, planets, and people), it should give us a sense of assurance. Someone is in control of this thing we call the universe. There is a purpose and there is a reason.

The next question we may ask is why create the Heavens and the Earth? We can tell by observing these two elements that God is into details. Everything has been made to precision, elegantly designed with the most robust systems locked in place. God takes His work seriously with the utmost respect and care. It is clear He takes pleasure in His work.

When we see His handiwork in the Heavens and the Earth, how can we look at ourselves and say He did not take the same time, care, and attention in creating us? It's not possible. We have observed the brilliance of His work around us. God has given life, form, function, beauty, and purpose to all things, and we are no exception.

WORD STUDY

In the beginning
בְּרֵאשִׁית
In Hebrew, this is **bə·rê·šîṯ**, which means the first, in place, time, order, rank

God
אֱלֹהִים
In Hebrew, this is **'ĕ·lō·hîm**, which means gods—the supreme God, magistrates, a superlative

created
בָּרָא
In Hebrew, this is **bā·rā**, which means to create, to cut down, select, feed

the heavens
הַשָּׁמַיִם
In Hebrew, this is **haš·šā·ma·yim**, which means Heaven, sky

the earth
הָאָרֶץ:
In Hebrew, this is **hā·'ā·reṣ**, which means Earth, land

PRAYER

Almighty God, I acknowledge you as the All-Powerful One. You are the Creator of the universe and the One who knows all things and is present everywhere at all times. You are Lord of lords, Great and Mighty and Awesome in all your ways. There is none to compare to you. I lift up praise to the greatness of who you are. Let my heart forever be filled with the wonder of you, and your praise forever be on my lips.

In Jesus' Name, Amen.

POEM

~

I shout for joy at the work of your hands,
The Faithful Creator who was there before time began.
The Heavens, Oh Lord, cannot contain you
The brilliance of you is immeasurable and incomprehensible.
Who is like unto our God?
All Glory, All splendour, All riches, All power
Praise to the King of kings and Lord of lords.
As we look all around us,
We see the handiwork of God.

It was yours in the beginning
And in the fullness of time,
You will gather together all things in Christ.
Everything on Earth and Everything in Heaven
Giving glory to God
God and Man dwelling together.

CHAPTER TWO: EXODUS

❧

MOSES

Exodus 5:22-23 (NKJV)

So Moses returned to the LORD and said, "Lord, why have You brought trouble on this people? Why is it You have sent me? For since I came to Pharaoh to speak in Your name, he has done evil to this people; neither have You delivered Your people at all.

THOUGHT

I cannot count the number of times I have started to pray about something for my family, and the exact opposite happened. It would freak me out! I began to seriously think I shouldn't pray because unbeknown to my family, I was the reason they were being afflicted with more suffering. And it wasn't fair on them because they were not Christians; therefore, they are not in a position to defend themselves against what was happening. I struggled with this thinking for YEARS. Then one day, I came across an article with this scripture. Have you ever gone to do something good and it seemed to backfire? Well, Moses had a similar problem, so I guess we're in good company. The very next chapter, God encourages Moses in six ways

1. God reassures Moses He will deal with Pharaoh and He will let the children of Israel go

2. God reminds Moses of who He is "...I am the LORD..."

3. God reminds Moses of His generational faithfulness by citing Moses forefathers in the faith.

4. God reminds Moses of His promise to give them the land of Canaan.

5. God reminds Moses He hears the cry of His people and remembers His covenant

6. God then instructs Moses to tell the children of Israel His name which is LORD, and of His promise to deliver them out of Egypt and bring them into their heritage.

What's my point?

Let's do what Moses did when things seem to go in the opposite direction to what God said and disappointment sets in. Moses went straight back to God for answers.

God did not chastise Moses for having questions or for his insecurity. God took the time to build up Moses' faith and encourage Him.

Let us return to God when our expectations seemed to be unmet. Don't walk away from God; walk to Him. Just think if Moses had quit and walked away, we would not have the

Exodus story. You have a story, waiting to be written as we continue to return to Him even in the face of contradictory reports.

WORD STUDY

LORD

יְהוָה

In Hebrew, this is **Yahweh**, which means LORD, the one
true God

Lord

אֲדֹנָי

In Hebrew, this is **Adonay**, which means Lord

Trouble

הֵרַע

In Hebrew, this is **hê·ra'**, which means to spoil

Pharoah

פַּרְעֹה

In Hebrew, this is **par·'ōh**, which means the title of Egyptian
kings

Delivered

וְהַצֵּל

In Hebrew, this is **wə·haṣ·ṣêl**, which means to strip, plunder,
deliver oneself, be delivered, snatch away, deliver

PRAYER

Lord Jesus, help me to see you at work in the most difficult of situations. Help me to believe you can change the hardest of hearts and the seemingly impossible circumstances. When I step out in faith, and the outcome does not meet my expectation, help me not to walk away in discouragement but return to you and seek you for answers. I trust in your promise that you willingly give wisdom to those who ask. Help me to trust and not doubt you even when situations look completely the opposite of what I'm believing for. Help me rehearse your promises, knowing you are trustworthy and cannot fail. You are well able to bring your promise to pass and so I praise and thank you in advance.

In Jesus' Name, Amen.

POEM

~

When doubt arises in my heart,
Let your word speak louder.
When the enemy throws his darts of doubt,
Your shield of faith is my cover.
When a cacophony of unbelief the world seeks to unleash,
Let God be true and His glory arise.
For in the victory of the cross I will abide.

CHAPTER THREE: DEUTERONOMY

BE STRONG

Deuteronomy 31:6 (NKJV)

Be strong and of good courage, do not fear nor be afraid of them; for the LORD your God, He is the One who goes with you. He will not leave you nor forsake you.

THOUGHT

*M*oses was one hundred and twenty years old; he had led the children of Israel as far as the Jordan River, and now, God was calling Him home. Joshua was to be their newly appointed leader. Under his leadership, Moses declared God's promise that they would defeat their enemies and claim territory. Only the people were to be strong and of good courage.

God has given us many promises in the Bible, and we all have ground to take back from our enemies and land to inherit. I mean this in every dimension of the word—physically, emotionally, relationally, financially, generationally, and spiritually.

The wealth available to us in Christ is beyond our imagination, and even the span of our lifetimes could never exhaust God's blessings.

In this scripture, God clearly tells us we have an enemy that wants to rob us of claiming what is ours and that enemy's name is fear.

I am a natural worrier; it doesn't take much happening in life for me to start feeling overwhelmed. My stomach starts churning, and my head feels tense. All my focus goes straight to the problem, and in those moments, it can be pretty hard to see straight or think clearly.

Thank goodness for the Holy Spirit and God's word to remind me in good days or bad. God's truth does not change. I can stand on what He said and not how I feel.

The enemy comes to steal, kill, and destroy. He attacks our minds with fear and doubts about who God is, what He said, and who we are.

God is our help, and through His powerful word, we have authority to chase those lies away. We fight from the position of Christ's victory.

Sometimes, the ground we fight for is our peace of mind. Sometimes, it's holding onto the truth that we are loved by God and have value and worth. Sometimes, it's holding on to the promise of our calling in Christ or believing God to open a door of opportunity or to sustain us amid a trial.

Whatever that sacred ground you are claiming, know that the Lord has already given it to you. Even when it feels overwhelming or unobtainable, remember God is the One who goes with you. He will not leave nor forsake you. God has equipped you to win every battle.

WORD STUDY

Be Strong
חזק

In Hebrew, it is **Chazaq**, which means strong, repair, hold, strengthen, encourage

Good Courage
אמץ

In Hebrew, this is **Amats**, which means courageous, establish, fortify, prevailed

The Lord
יְהוָה

In Hebrew, this is **Yah·weh**, which means Lord, God, Jehovah

God
אֱלֹהֶיךָ

In Hebrew, this is **ĕ·lō·he·ḵā**, which means God, judge

Leave
יַרְפְּךָ

In Hebrew, this is **yar·pə·ḵā**, which means God, judge

Forsake
יַעַזְבֶךָ׃

In Hebrew, this is **ya·ʿaz·ḇe·kā**, which means to loose,
relinquish, permit

PRAYER

Lord Jesus, when I'm facing storms in my life, when fear threatens to overwhelm me, overwhelm me with your perfect love that casts out all fear. Give me faith to boldly speak your truth over my life and the situation. Help me stand on the promise of your word and not give up. Help me to keep trusting you, knowing you are the author and finisher of my faith.

In Jesus' Name, Amen.

POEM

~

Be strong and of good courage,
But my heart is filled with fear.
Previews of misfortune,
Fill my mind and steal my peace.
The enemy of my soul,
Deadens hope with his torment.

But you are the resurrection and the life,
You cause my hope to live again.

Jesus comes that I might have life
And have it more abundantly;
The Helper comes to comfort me
And quickens your word to me;
You shall live and shall not die,
I am your hope; I heard you cry,
Your battles you will never fight alone,
For I am Your victory, Your courage, Your God

CHAPTER FOUR: JUDGES

GIDEON

Judges 7:2 (NKJV)

And the Lord said to Gideon, "The people who are with you are too many for Me to give the Midianites into their hands, lest Israel claim glory for itself against Me, saying, 'My own hand has saved me."

THOUGHT

*C*utbacks are tough but necessary in life. If we want to grow, every so often, we have to stop and evaluate ourselves. What direction is my life heading? Am I on the right track? Am I reading the right books? Am I accessing the relevant resources? Am I hanging around the right people that are going to help me succeed in life?

If the answer is no, it's time to make some adjustments.

The really tough calls are when you have to walk away from people. It's been said people come into your life for a reason, a season, or for life.

However, not every time of moving on has to be traumatic. In this scripture, we see God is the One deciding who will go with Gideon and who will not.

Perhaps Gideon thought in order to get the job done, he needed all the bells and whistles and manpower going. But the majority of these men were not fit for purpose, and God knew it. It was time to downsize.

With God, there is no uncertainty. He never says take this, just in case. God has already gone before us and knows what we will need before we even ask.

Weeds of pride and idolatry can take us by surprise when we don't guard our hearts. We experience some good fortune, and we start to think, did I do that? Did my own strength, intelligence, networking, qualifications or my own hand save me?

How quickly one wrong thought can blind and rob us of who is really blessing our lives?

When God says it's time to let go of something or someone, trust that He has better in store. Trust Him that He is doing it for our good and the outcome will be God being glorified and we being edified.

WORD STUDY

The LORD

יְהוָֹה

In Hebrew, this is **Yahweh**, which means the LORD —the
proper name of the God of Israel

too many

רַב

In Hebrew, this is **rab**, which means much, many, great

glorify themselves

יִתְפָּאֵר

In Hebrew, this is **yiṭ·pā·'êr**, which means to gleam, embellish,
to boast, to explain, oneself, to shake a, tree

has delivered

הוֹשִׁיעָה

In Hebrew, this is **hō·wō·šî·'āh**, which means to be open, wide,
free, to be safe, to free, succour

PRAYER

Heavenly Father, help me to trust you when you lead me to let things go in my life. Sometimes, I hold on to the past, people, or things so tight that it's hard to let them go when you say it's time. Help me trust you that you always have good things in store for me. The removal of something is not a loss but a setup for victory. Help me to focus on that and to give you all the glory when I win my battles.

In Jesus' Name, Amen.

POEM

~

My life was weighed down by so many things;
I thought I had to carry unforgiveness, anxiety, envy, resentment,
Disappointment, suffering, and sadness.
Then you came and showed me life did not have to be a burden
You took the weight of my sin and
Clothed me in righteousness and hope within;
Now I carry faith and love
Which are not weights at all
But treasures that delight my soul
And makes life's journey
A path of Hope

CHAPTER FIVE: 1 CHRONICLES

JABEZ

---

1 Chronicles 4:10 (NKJV)

And Jabez called on the God of Israel saying, "Oh, that You would bless me indeed, and enlarge my territory, that Your hand would be with me, and that You would keep me from evil, that I may not cause pain!" So God granted him what he requested.

THOUGHT

*T*here have been times in my life where I have felt like Jabez. I was convinced that I was toxic; everything I touched was tainted and ruined. The enemy of my soul had me convinced that I was good for nothing and had nothing to offer. Diverse ways to end my life would swirl around in my imagination. I would cry out to God in my anguish; why did you make me? Much later, I found similar cries in the Book of Job and Jeremiah 20:18. Then for a season, I found myself praying 1

Chronicles 4:10 also known as the Jabez prayer, and these words became the prayer of my heart.

It really moves me to come across people in the Bible, expressing the real rawness of their human experience to God. I struggled for years to express certain feelings to Him when I was growing up. Yes, I could worship Him and express adoration and praise, but there were other parts of my soul that needed a voice and God's healing. I had to borrow other people's words to fill my own. I still do sometimes, be at a song or book.

The intense emotion of Jabez's cry to the Lord is both harrowing and heart-rending. It was a cry of anguish and sorrow, and it was a cry for mercy.

It was a cry only God could answer, and He did.

The Bible gives us permission to come to God and pour out heart to Him without fear. We really can trust Him with all our hearts. So, come in authenticity and sincerity to your Saviour, He will hear your deepest hearts cry. He wants us to come to Him, and He will do for us what only He can do. He will turn our lives from pain to blessing

WORD STUDY

Called Out
וַיִּקְרָא

In Hebrew, this is **way·yiq·rā**, which means to call, proclaim, read

You would bless me
בֵּרֵךְ

In Hebrew, this is **bā·rêk**, which means to kneel, to bless God, man, to curse

and enlarge
וְהִרְבִּיתָ

In Hebrew, this is **wə·hir·bi·ṭā**, which means to be or become much, many or great

my territory!
גְּבוּלִי

In Hebrew, this is **gə·ḇū·lî**, which means a cord, a boundary, the territory inclosed

so that I will be free
לְבִלְתִּי

In Hebrew, this is **lə·ḇil·tî**, which means a failure of, not, except, without, unless, besides, because not, until

PRAYER

Dear Lord Jesus, sometimes we are just overwhelmed with our situations, and other times with our own selves. Everywhere we look, we see pain in us and around us, and it feels like we cannot escape it. Help Jesus to run to you, knowing you will never leave nor forsake us. Overwhelm us with your love, give us songs of deliverance and hear the cry of our hearts today. Change our narrative, write a new story for us, bless us, increase us, be with us, keep us, and make our lives a joy to others and a wonder to behold that testifies of your goodness.

In Jesus' Name, Amen.

POEM

~

No greater wonder to behold,
than God's love here in my soul.
Who is like the Lord to me!?
God who saves a wretch like me.
Who takes my ashes and beauty I receive.
All praise to God my redeemer lives.

CHAPTER SIX: NEHEMIAH

❧

REBUILD

Nehemiah 2:5 (NKJV)

And I said to the king, "If it pleases the king, and if your servant has found favour in your sight, I ask that you send me to Judah, to the city of my fathers' tombs, that I may rebuild it."

THOUGHT

*I*f you live long enough, you will experience times in your life that feel like a defining moment to do something significant. You will see or hear of something that produces a strength of feeling in you that compels you to action. It doesn't have to be on a big platform but something that makes a difference to somebody else.

My point is, we will find ourselves being a Nehemiah in someone's life, an opportunity to partner with God and see Him restore and rebuild the ruins of a wounded soul. Nehemiah was distressed at hearing the news that Jerusalem's temple had been left in ruin. The temple was significant to Israel; it was considered God's house, and it was a symbol of hope to the Jewish Nation. For it to be left in ruins was a reflection on the brokenness of its people.

Such news moved Nehemiah to act. His determination kept him focused on fending off bullies and critics who tried to strongly oppose his mission, but he was not deterred and finished the temple in a record of 52 days.

When we are spurred into action, we can accomplish great things on the back of that momentum. When God gives us favour for a task like He did for Nehemiah, we do not have to fear any opposition that comes against our righteous cause, for God is with us and will give us a great victory.

WORD STUDY

has found favor

יִיטַב

In Hebrew, this is **yî·ṭaḇ**, which means to be good, well, glad, or pleasing

so that I may rebuild it."

וְאֶבְנֶנָּה:

In Hebrew, this is (**wə·'eḇ·nen·nāh**), which means to build

PRAYER

Lord Jesus,

Thank you for the example of Nehemiah in scripture. His confidence and character are an example to me that you have given me favour and strength to fulfil the calling on my life.

Help me to be a Nehemiah, just like he was compelled to rebuild the walls of Jerusalem.

Let me look and see people the way you do. Where life has broken their walls down, give me the words and wisdom to speak your love, grace, and hope to them.

Father, use me to help rebuild the broken places in others, so that they will know there is a God who sees them and cares about them deeply.

Thank you for the restoration process in my life, my family, and those around me.

In Jesus' Name. Amen.

POEM

~

Broken places, broken dreams, identity stolen, crumbling
possibilities.
Life had dealt me blow after blow,
I thought I was strong, but situations took their toll.
I made some bad decisions and I have some regrets.
Guilt and compromise left me vulnerable to attack
My walls kept crumbling, crumbling down.
But Jesus, my true Nehemiah, rebuilt my life on solid ground.

Lord, raise up Nehemiah's that will be vessels of honour.
Willing to reach other people who are broken,
Those society overlooks but who are not beyond your sight.
Lord, I ask you to restore and rebuild their lives
And in them let your glory reside.

CHAPTER SEVEN: ESTHER

WE HAVE VICTORY

Esther 8:11 (NLT)

The king's decree gave the Jews in every city authority to unite to defend their lives. They were allowed to kill, slaughter, and annihilate anyone of any nationality or province who might attack them or their children and wives, and to take the property of their enemies.

THOUGHT

*N*ear the end of the Book of Esther, the Jewish people are living under the threat of annihilation. Haman's hatred for Mordecai has grown so wildly out of control; his solution for getting rid of Mordecai is to wipe out all the Jewish people. Haman had manipulated the King in Esther Chapter 3 into handing over his signet ring so he could write this decree.

In a series of miraculous events, the plot is discovered, Haman is hanged, and Mordecai promoted. In those days, when a law was passed using the King's signet ring, it could not be revoked, but Mordecai was able to use the King's ring to write a new decree. God's people could arm themselves and fight on the day of battle, and God gave His people victory over their enemies.

Haman could be seen as a type of Satan. From the beginning, he deceived Adam and Eve and took their authority. Now, humanity lives with the impact of sin all around us. Jesus, as the perfect man, conquered sin and took back humanity's authority. Now, Jesus has given that authority back to us to defeat sin and use our authority over Satan in Jesus' name. Jesus stripped the enemy of his ability to use sin as a means to steal, kill, and destroy us. Jesus has armed us with all we need to win our battles.

We still have to fight, but we fight from the place of victory!

Just like the King's decree gave the Jews the authority to fight and God gave them the victory. Our Heavenly King has given us authority to defend ourselves. When we feel like the enemy is encroaching on our territory. Use the Word of God to fight back. Find the promises of God that speak to your situation be it your health, finances, a relationships issue.

So, when you go to battle, go with confidence and in the strength of your victorious God.

WORD STUDY

Permitted

נָתַן

In Hebrew, this is **nā·ṯan**, which means to give, put, set

and defend

עַל-

In Hebrew, this is **'al-**, which means above, over, upon, against

and to plunder

וּשְׁלָלָם

In Hebrew, this is **ū·šə·lā·lām**, which means a prey, spoil, plunder, booty

PRAYER

Lord Jesus, thank you that you have already defeated Satan, conquered him, and given us the authority to use your name. Help me to be courageous in pursuing you and all you have for me. Help me to rise above my limitations and claim my inheritance in Christ. Teach me how to use the spiritual weapons you have given me and help me to be the overcomer and more than a conqueror you created me to be.

In Jesus' Name. Amen.

POEM

~

You fought my greatest battle and defeated my biggest foe
Disarmed rulers and authorities
Made them an open show
You sent your Holy Spirit
To live inside of me
Your Blood, Word, and Spirit
The power that set me free.
Teach me to renew my mind
Teach me who I am
Teach me Lord to walk with you
And fulfil your perfect plan.

CHAPTER EIGHT: PSALMS

EXPECTATION

Psalm 62:5 (NKJV)

My soul, wait silently for God alone, For my expectation is from Him.

THOUGHT

*C*oming to Christ is all about an uplifted life.

It's all over the Bible; we have been seated in heavenly places. We lay up our treasure in Heaven; we set our affections on things above. God does exceedingly abundantly above. We look to the hills, where our help comes from.

Even John the Revelator was told to "come up" in the Book of Revelation for God to show Him things to come.

We are always encouraged to look up.

When we have an expectation, it means we have hope for some future promises. Our hope is rock solid because it is anchored in God. The expectation is a strong belief that something will happen. God has given all of us good "somethings" to look forward to in His word. God says He knows the plans He has for us. We don't have to wait anxiously, fretting before the Lord, but rather our soul can be silent. It can be at rest because our soul knows we are cherished, seen, and loved.

WORD STUDY

O my soul

נַפְשִׁי

In Hebrew, this is **nap̄·šî**, which means a soul, living being, life, self, person, desire, passion, appetite, emotion

my hope

תִּקְוָתִי:

In Hebrew, this is **tiq·wā·tî**, which means a cord, expectancy

PRAYER

Heavenly Father, thank you for your love for me. I bring my soul to you, you who can calm any storm. When I am flustered, worried or stressed, I know if I can just come into your presence, you will cause my soul to rest. Lord, I can wait well in confidence because you are the promise-keeping God. What you have spoken, you are able to bring it to pass. Help me to wait patiently, knowing that your timing in my life is perfect.

In Jesus' Name, Amen.

POEM

~

In your presence Lord, I find peace.
In you there is no rushing, fretting, or stressing.
For you are timeless and you redeem the time.
When I feel frustrated with the pace of life,
You prove time and time again you are never late
Always on time.
So, let my soul wait silently for you
My confidence assured
You are not a man that you should lie
You have the words of eternal life
Unbreakable, unshakeable
Your word does not return void
It is the anchor of my soul
It is the path to my eternal home.

CHAPTER NINE: PSALMS

THE WORD IS LIGHT

Psalms 119:105 (NKJV)

Your word is a lamp to my feet and a light to my path.

THOUGHT

One of the hardest places to find ourselves is in the valley of uncertainty.

To use another example, it's like a 10,000 piece jigsaw puzzle where only a third of it is complete. There are still so many gaps and perhaps a couple of pieces you just jammed in to fit out of frustration, which you know you'll have to deal with later.

It's such an opportunity to doubt, become confused and insecure about yourself, life, and everything. You can't see the whole picture, and it's frustrating the socks off you.

We get into reasoning and try to figure things out in our heads and then feel like God's holding out on us. "Give us the details already; I can handle it".

Then, after the tantrum and coming to our senses, He speaks!

Don't you love that! (Not the tantrums) I don't know about you, but my fragile little heart still longs to know that papa God sees me and cares. He may not give me all the answers I want, but He always gives me exactly what I need—enough light for the next step.

WORD STUDY

is a lamp

נֵר־

In Hebrews, this is **nêr-**, which means a lamp, light

to my feet

לְרַגְלִי

In Hebrews, this is **lə·raḡ·li**, which means a foot, a step, the pudenda

and a light

וְאֹור

In Hebrew, this is **wə·'ō·wr**, which means Illumination, luminary

PRAYER

Heavenly Father,

Sometimes, I get frustrated when I can't see the full picture. I become impatient and get myself worked up into a frazzle. You are so kind to come alongside and speak calm to the wind and waves of my busy mind and billowing emotions. You come and shine your light so I can see the next step to take and it becomes all I need to keep going.

Thank you for your faithfulness; it is better than life to me.

In Jesus' Name, Amen.

POEM

~

In you there is no shifting shadow
No dark side is there to you
You dwell in unapproachable light
Whom no man has seen or can see;
Your life is the light of men
Light to all mankind
God who commanded light to shine
Out of darkness
Has shone in our hearts to give
The glory of God in the face of Jesus Christ.

CHAPTER TEN: PSALMS

THE WORD

Psalms 119 (NKJV)

V5 Oh that my ways were directed to keep your statutes!

V10... Oh let me not wander from Your commandments

V27 Make me understand the way of Your precepts...

V34 Give me understanding and I shall keep your law.

V35 Make me walk in the path of your commandments...

V36 Incline my heart to your testimonies and not to covetousness.

V37 Turn away my eyes from looking at worthless things...

V40 ...Revive me in your righteousness

V73 ...Give me understanding that I may learn your commandments

V107 ...Revive me oh Lord according to your word

V116 Uphold me according to your word, that I may live....

V117 Hold me up and I shall be safe...

THOUGHT

*a*s I read Psalm 119, I began to notice something about the psalmist. He was constantly asking God to make him what He was not. He recognised that if he was going to be any kind of witness for God, He had better ask God to help him every step of the way. There is a longing and yearning for God that comes through the pages. The psalmist is not riddled with guilt and woe is me-ism, but is rather fervent in his pursuit of God.

I was reminded of a similar passage of scripture in Galatians chapter 3, where the Apostle Paul said;

"Are you so foolish? Having begun in the Spirit, are you now being made perfect by the flesh?"

Our sin, weaknesses and failures point to why we need a Saviour, and how much we need His daily help. God is not shocked and ashamed of our ineptness at living for Him. That's why He came, to save us and to give us His Holy Spirit to empower us to live right.

So, let's not be bashful but bold like the Psalmist and ask God for all we need to live this Christian life.

WORD STUDY

my heart
לִבִּי

In Hebrews, this is **lib·bî**, which means the heart, the feelings,
the will, the intellect, centre

from worthless things;
שָׁוְא

In Hebrew, this is **šāw**, which means evil, idolatry, uselessness

that I may live;
וְאֶחְיֶה

In Hebrew, this is **wə·'eḥ·yeh**, which means to live, to revive

Uphold me,
סְעָדֵנִי

In Hebrew, this is **sə·'ā·ḏê·nî**, which means to support, sustain,
and stay

PRAYER

Lord Jesus, you are the vine and I am the branch. In your wisdom, you told me to abide in you because apart from you, I can do nothing. Oh Lord, how true I find these words to be daily. So, I join with the Psalmist and ask you to make me what I'm not. When I don't love like you, Lord Jesus, change my heart. When I don't want to be patient or compassionate, Lord Jesus, make me over. When my pride and selfishness get the best of me, Jesus, increase me in love and humility. Revive me in you; refresh me in you. Put a new desire and passion in me for you, for the Kingdom of God and others today.

In Jesus' Name, Amen.

POEM

~

When my fire is burning low and my love is growing cold
When my heart is feeling hard and I feel like giving up
Take me quickly to my Saviour to perform His divine operation
And engraft His word into my soul,
To give a joyful heart for these dry bones.
Let me drink His living water,
For despair you give me hope,
For my mourning you give me gladness,
And beauty for my ashes,
My transformation is complete,
Restore my faith so I can see
His perfect love is all I need,
The Great Physician has healed me.

CHAPTER ELEVEN: PSALMS

MATTERS OF THE HEART

Psalm 119:36 (NKJV)

Incline my heart your testimonies. And not to covetousness.

THOUGHT

*O*ne day, I was talking to God about my heart. I kept feeling like a war was going on internally, literally in my heart, with all sorts of ugly issues coming up; it was disturbing and disconcerting.

I asked God, what's wrong with me?

Was He saying ALL these issues were in my heart?

Was the enemy trying to trick me to make me feel like these issues were mine when they weren't.

(This has happened to me before.)

. . .

Earlier in the week I felt led to revisit Psalm 119 every so often. During one particular reading I felt led to highlight all the places where it said "whole heart", another time to highlight the word "testimony" and it was in verse 36 I felt led to stop and ponder.

Psalm 119:36 (NKJV)

Incline my heart to your testimonies. And not to covetousness.

I started talking to God about my heart. I said, "God there's something here I need to see, your word is giving me a remedy here". As I read it again thoughts began to form in my mind. "I'm not to be covetous but rather delight in your testimonies".

I have this way of praying sometimes where I'm just talking to God and then I shift to declaring God's word back to Him and petitioning and then go back to talking to Him and asking questions.

I couldn't read past Psalm 119 verse 36, and as I was talking the Holy Spirit was giving me understanding. I was not to desire what other people experienced but instead to change my heart attitude. I was to rejoice with those who rejoice. I started to pray *"Lord help me to do this. If I can't celebrate with others why should anyone celebrate with me. Make me generous of heart, not insecure but delight in seeing my brother and sister receive their breakthrough, their healing, their prophetic word, their blessing. Help me to mourn with those who mourn and rejoice with those who rejoice".*

Then I meditated on the word 'testimonies'. A testimony is someone recounting their experience with the Lord Jesus. They are sharing their story of who Jesus is and how He showed up in their life. It's not only a revelation of who God is but what He can do.

I felt that I was to delight in hearing the stories of what Jesus was doing in the lives of others, I was to incline my heart to them. I should lean into them with a heart attitude of delight and be encouraged and an assured that I serve a God who keeps His promises.

Doing this will help to guard my heart against coveting, envy and jealousy. I'm to be captivated watching how our heavenly father moves and touches the lives of people. I'm watching Papa at work and learning His ways. What can be more wonderful than watching the Spirit of Christ at work.

WORD STUDY

Turn

הַט־

In Greek, this is **hat-** which means to stretch out, spread out, extend, incline, bend

my heart

לִבִּי

In Greek, this is **lib·bî,** which means the heart, the feelings, the will, the intellect, centre

PRAYER

Lord shape my heart to delight in hearing the stories of your greatness and of who you are. Make me generous of heart. Help me to mourn with those who mourn and rejoice with those who rejoice.

Amen

POEM

Shape my heart to love your stories
Incline my heart to your testimonies
As my heart is filled with who you are
Hope is birthed and lies are starved
The testimony of Jesus is the Spirit of Prophecy
Declaring the wonder of God and His glory
What He does for one He will do for you
So hope in God and expect Him to move.

CHAPTER TWELVE: PSALMS

WONDERFULLY MADE

Psalm 139:14 (NKJV)

I will praise You, for I am fearfully and wonderfully made; Marvellous are Your works, And that my soul knows very well.

THOUGHT

J remember one evening, sitting on my couch at home and bursting into tears. I had been feeling particularly low that day, so I started reading through my Bible confessions. I could not get past this verse of scripture in Psalms 139. God ministered to my heart through His word, letting me know I had value and worth. As I meditated on the verse, in my heart, I was imagining God creating me and shaping me to be exactly how He wanted me to be. And in that moment, God's word came alive in my heart.

Our enemy (the devil) wants us to feel so awful about ourselves that we'll give up doing anything for God because we'll think it has no value because we have none. My friend…

It's a big fat lie from the devil.

I encourage you, any time you feel diminished or lacking in your self-worth, find those Bible verses that tell you who you are in God. God's word is true, no matter how you feel or what kind of day you've had. His love for you never changes.

Take your time and read the definitions of this scripture below. It's God reminding you of who you are. I've taken these meanings and turned them into prayer at the end. Feel free to pray this prayer as you agree with who God says you are.

WORD STUDY

Praise
אוֹדְךָ

In Hebrew, this is **Yadhah**, which means to throw, cast. To speak out, confess; to praise. To sing, to give thanks.

Fearfully
נוֹרָאוֹת

In Hebrew, this is **Yare**, which means to be reverenced, a positive feeling of awe or reverence.

Wonderfully
נִפְלֵיתִי

In Hebrew, this is **Palah** which means distinguish, put a difference, show marvellous, separate, set apart, sever, make wonderful

Marvellous
נִפְלֵיתִי

In Hebrew, this is **Pala**, which means to be separate, be distinguished, be extraordinary, be wonderful, act miraculously, act marvellously, to sanctify, wondrous things, miracles

Works
מַעֲשֶׂיךָ

In Hebrew, this is **Maaseka,** which means an action, transaction, activity, product, property,

Soul
וְנַפְשִׁי
In Hebrew, this is **Nephesh**, which means a breathing creature (man or animal) life, soul, spirit and mind.

Know
יָדַעַת
In Hebrew, this is **Yadha**, which means to perceive, understand, acquire knowledge, know discern, be acquainted.

Very well
מְאֹד:
In Hebrew, this is **me od**, which means muchness, force, abundance

PRAYER

Lord Jesus, I praise you because when you made me, you created me with such reverence and tenderness because I am precious to you.

You took care and you took time making sure my every detail was perfect.

I am distinguished, different, and unique.

You created me to be extraordinary and that's what I am.

I am your marvellous work, full of wonder, miracles, and your beauty.

I know this, I receive this, I believe this, I live this.

My soul is rich, wealthy, and abundant in this truth.

In Jesus' Name, Amen.

POEM

~

Looking in the mirror
What do I see?
Flaws and disappointments?
Regrets of what might have been?
An image to despise?
A failure not worth the time?

It's time to smash the mirror of lies.

In the mirror of God's Word
My true identity is defined
My mistakes God takes
In their place a new life
As I fix my eyes on Him
My life looks more like His.

CHAPTER THIRTEEN: PROVERBS

WISE CORRECTION

Proverbs 15:31-32 (NLT)

If you listen to constructive criticism, you will be at home among the wise.

If you reject discipline, you only harm yourself; but if you listen to correction, you grow in understanding.

THOUGHT

*O*ne of the hardest times to stay committed to being your best self is when life hurts. Maybe you took a risk on an idea and it backfired, or a loved one let you down, or you went out of your way to do something helpful for someone and your gesture wasn't well received. In fact, the person wasn't thankful but critical of your actions.

It's easy to throw your hands in the air and say, what's the point?

Truth is, the last example that recently happened to me. The critical comment just kept playing on my mind over and over. I kept trying to give myself pep talks *"...be resilient J; you know you meant well."* In reality, I felt hurt and deflated. As I was dwelling on the situation suddenly, a wave of memories washed over me, reminding me of other critical comments directed at me.

This sensation did not stir up self-pity but rather questions, I willed myself to choose self-reflection instead of mental self-flagellation. "I can grow from this", I told myself. I want to be 'a' better person not 'the' better person, as the latter would imply viewing my experience as someone being right and the other wrong.

In that moment, I chose to focus on seeing both sides of my experience and how I could respond in a healthy way.

When negative thoughts could have carried me down an all too familiar path, I decided to focus on how to be my best self.

In those moments, when negative experiences want to drag you down, remind yourself what matters most to you. Remember the person you want to be and who you are, even when that's misunderstood. In other words, FOCUS on what will help you keep moving forward.

WORD STUDY

life-giving

חַיִּים

In Hebrew, this is ḥay·yîm, which means alive, raw, fresh,
strong, life

reproof

תּוֹכַחַת

In Hebrew, this is tō·w·ḵa·ḥat, which means chastisement,
correction, refutation, proof
but whoever heeds

וְשׁוֹמֵעַ

In Hebrew, this is wə·šō·w·mê·a', which means to hear
intelligently

correction

תּוֹכַחַת

In Hebrew, this is tō·w·ḵa·ḥat, which means chastisement,
correction, refutation, proof

gains

קוֹנֶה

In Hebrew, this is qō·w·neh, which means to erect, create, to
procure, by purchase, to own

understanding

לֵב:

In Hebrew, this is **lêḇ**, which means the heart, the feelings, the will, the intellect, centre

PRAYER

Lord Jesus, help me to be humble, to listen to constructive criticism without becoming defensive. Help me, Lord, to be open to change. Let me not be quick to retaliate or hide in self-pity, but be willing to listen and learn about where I need to change. Help me, Lord, to do so.

In Jesus' Name, Amen.

POEM

When I feel misunderstood, chastised, or overlooked
Lord, help my soul to not shrink back
But give me the courage to listen and learn
When I feel crushed and a little despondent
When words are said that leave me wondering
Let me bring it all to you and pray
Heal my heart and hear the truth
Give me the strength to change and lay down my selfish ways
Help me to surrender
Make me more like Christ within.

CHAPTER FOURTEEN: PROVERBS

TREASURE HUNT

Proverbs 25:2 (NLT)

It is God's privilege to conceal things and the king's privilege to discover them.

THOUGHT

*T*here was a time when I would read the Bible, and if something did not make sense to me, I would question, *"Oh, why the discrepancy????"*

Then one day, a thought came to me, that I should trust what I already know to be true of God's nature and His Word. I should think, there is something here I do not understand yet, so I should ask God about it and then wait for Him to reveal the truth to me in His time.

We should not let what may seem to be a discrepancy, pull us away from the truth of God's Word. Let's ask God to show us the deeper truths until that "seeming discrepancy" lines up with **THE TRUTH**.

In the Bible, Jesus would sometimes talk to people in parables and then take His disciples aside to explain things more clearly to them.

Proverbs 25:2: It is the glory of God to conceal a matter, but the glory of kings is to search out a matter.

God is not hiding things from us because they are not ours. Rather, He is hiding things for us to discover.

The Bible is full of treasures. Just like diamonds are hidden deep in the earth, the richest truths require us to spend time with God and His Word before we understand them.

Are we up for a treasure hunt?

WORD STUDY

It is the glory

כָּבֵד

In Hebrew, this is **kə·ḇōḏ**, which means weight, splendour, copiousness

to conceal

הַסְתֵּר

In Hebrew, this means **has·têr**, which means to hide, conceal

to search it out.

חֵקֶר

In Hebrew, this is **ḥǎ·qōr**, which means to penetrate, to examine intimately

PRAYER

Thank you, Lord, that you have great spiritual treasures for me to discover. Help me to be diligent and stay motivated to keep asking, seeking, and knocking. Thrill my heart, Oh Lord! Let me be delighted by you as I pursue you as you pursue my heart. May I rejoice in knowing the riches of your love all the more.

In Jesus' Name, Amen.

POEM

Your ways unsearchable, your love unfathomable
Yet still I am drawn to seek,
to discover more of you
to learn and to know you
Oh Lord, it's your wisdom I need.
The more I learn of you, the more I yearn for you
You make life worth living for me.
As deep calls to deep
Immersed in you I'm complete
Your wonders I behold
Lost in your divine flow.

CHAPTER FIFTEEN: ST MATTHEW

IDENTITY

Matthew 4:3-4 (NKJV)

Now when the tempter came to Him, he said, "If You are the Son of God, command that these stones become bread."

But He answered and said, "It is written, 'Man shall not live by bread alone, but by every word that proceeds from the mouth of God."

THOUGHT

One of Satan's tactics is to create confusion about your identity. One particular week, I sensed being under spiritual attacks. My emotions were all over the place, and I felt spiritually far from God. My sleep was disturbed, and I had an overwhelming feeling of despair. It lasted about a week and afterwards, I felt like I had gone a few rounds in the boxing ring and my soul was worse for wear. In all honesty, I was upset with God. Where were you in all this? I thought you were my protector? I felt blindsided. I'm supposed to be safe with you? My questions were heartfelt, but the enemy took the opportunity to play on my insecurities. Does God really care about me?

That Sunday, our Co-Pastor, Marie, preached a word on shutting out the negative voices and people in your life. I realised that's what I needed to do. My experience had me doubting the goodness of God and His character. I had a choice to allow my experience to change what was true of God, or trust that He was good, and there was more to my experience than what I currently understood. As I made the choice to turn to Him, He shone His light in my heart and gave me vital insight through His word that spoke hope and healing to my soul.

His word became my sword to win the battle against the enemy. Jesus did the same; He used the Word of God to defeat Satan.

Even through the heat of our battles, God is always our victory banner.

WORD STUDY

tempter
πειράζων
In Greek, this is **peirazōn**, which means to try, tempt, test. From peira; to test, i.e. Endeavor, scrutinize, entice, discipline

[the] Son
Υἱὸς
In Greek, this is **Huios**, which means a son, descendent. Apparently, a primary word; a 'son', used very widely of immediate, remote or figuratively, kinship

of God
Θεοῦ
In Greek, this is **Theou**, which is a deity, especially the supreme divinity; figuratively, a magistrate; by Hebraism, very

PRAYER

Dear God, sometimes when I'm going through hard times, the longer it goes on, the wearier I become. It can seem like the rage of the storm and the oppressive dark clouds block me from seeing you and me wonder if I really am alone. Help me to put my faith in your word and not my experience. It is through your word you promised to anchor me. Through your word, you remind me I am loved, seen, and I belong to you. Let my heart never draw away from you in tough times, but help me to draw nearer. Hide me, Lord, in your unfailing love.

In Jesus' Name, Amen.

POEM

~

Lord, your word is my defence,
It is my shield, my daily bread,
It is the truth on which I stand.
It reminds me of who I am,
Tells me your salvation plan,
Victory ground on which I stand.
A life no longer bound by sin
But liberated to serve, worship, and live,
Eternally with the King of kings.

CHAPTER SIXTEEN: ST MATTHEW

$\mathcal{C\!\!\!\!\!\!\!\!\infty}$

THE LIGHT LIFE

Matthew 6:22 (NLT)

"Your eye is like a lamp that provides light for your body. When your eye is healthy, your whole body is filled with light".

THOUGHT

*M*any years ago, I volunteered with a charity called Compassion UK. I attended an Amy Grant concert *(Amy Grant is an American Grammy award-winning-singer-songwriter).*

As I listened to this super-talented musician, something almost mystical radiated from her. I realised I was watching someone who was being their truest self and doing exactly what they were born to do, and it was mesmerising.

Figuring out our truest self can be a journey of ups and downs, missteps, and Ah-ha! Moments.

We have all done jobs we disliked and were not the best use of our abilities, and if we stay in those places longer than we should, those experiences could impact our soul and how we see ourselves.

Picture it like this, for every part of your soul, you can express your true authentic self, you light up. And for the parts where life oppresses you, it's like your light is diminished.

Has anyone ever said to you, *"You light up when you talk about..."* You fill in the blank.

Why is that?

I believe that when we tap into what truly makes us tick, we literally light up from the inside and people can see it in our talk, posture, and attitude. We come alive!

When we show up as authentic, we affect those around us. Your life will broadcast at a frequency that says, I know who I am and what I'm about. You'll love me or hate me, but you cannot be indifferent to me. You are either drawn to the light in my life or repelled by it, but you cannot be unaffected (John 3:20, 21).

Only God can reveal to us who we truly are; life in the grey zone, or the dark, is not for any of us. We were made for more; we were all made to light up the world around us, so don't let anything or anyone dim who God made you be. Keep shining for Jesus.

WORD STUDY

lamp
λύχνος
In Greek, this is **lychnos**, which means a lamp. From the base of leukos; a portable lamp or other illuminator

vision
ὀφθαλμός
In Greek, this is **ophthalmos**, which means the eye; fig: the mind's eye. From optanomai; the eye; by implication, vision; figuratively, envy

full of light
φωτεινὸν
In Greek, this is **phōteinon**, which means bright, luminous, full of light. From phos; lustrous, i.e., Transparent or well-illuminated

PRAYER

Jesus, you are the light of the world and all mankind.

You made me a child of light and not of darkness.

Help me never to entertain unfruitful works of darkness but to walk in line with your Word.

Empower me to follow you, so that I will always see which way to go and my footing will be sure.

Let my life shine brightly for you Lord,

In Jesus' Name

Amen.

POEM

～

You lit up creation when you said let there be light;
Your every word full of eternal life,
Always shine in our hearts to give us the light,
Of the knowledge
Of the glory of God
In the face of Jesus Christ.

CHAPTER SEVENTEEN: ST MATTHEW

FIND REST

Matthew 11:28 (NKJV)

Come to Me, all you who labour and are heavy laden, and I will give you rest.

THOUGHT

*H*uman beings were not created to walk through life's ups and downs alone. Jesus says when you are feeling weary in life, when you feel heavy and weighed down by the cares of life or the weight of the world is on your shoulders, come to Jesus, you can exchange your weariness for His rest.

Jesus is the good shepherd; He knows how to give you rest and what type of rest you need. Rest can be taking us out of something or taking us into something. It can take us out of a lengthy trial into a season of favour.

Rest can mean more sleep, more recreation time. It can be rest from an intense season of work. Sometimes, our soul finds rest in a community or a certain quality of friendship. When I was going through a rough season, God brought a very sanguine friend into my life to balance out the heaviness in me. That was rest for my soul.

Jesus wants to take care of you if you let Him. He is the burden-bearer; He can lift the burden off you through prayer and He can lift it through community and fellowship with others. Hand your cares over to Jesus and watch Him work out your every care.

WORD STUDY

are weary
κοπιῶντες
In Greek, this is **kopiōntes**, which means, from a derivative of
kopos; to feel fatigue; by implication, to work hard

.

burdened,
πεφορτισμένοι
In Greek, this is **pephortismenoi**, which means to load, burden;
pass: To be laden. From phortos; to load up, i.e. to overburden
with ceremony

will give you rest
ἀναπαύσω
In Greek, this is **anapausō**, which means from ana and pauo; to
repose (be exempt), remain); by implication, to refresh

PRAYER

Precious Jesus, thank you. When I'm weary and going through a tough time, you understand. You are touched by the things that touch my soul. You care about all my cares, the people who have hurt me, the losses I'm going through, a sickness I'm facing, and a troubled relationship. Father, I lay before you all my concerns, and I ask you to refresh me and renew my strength.

Help me to be still and know that you are God.

In Jesus' name. Amen.

POEM

~

Rest is what I find in thee
A place to lay every worry
No rest like yours can this world offer
You restore my soul
With your living water.
I thought my soul was wild and free
I did not know it needed thee;
My soul was tethered to a heavy harness
I bear the marks of cruel taskmasters.
Finally, I am ready to listen and yield
And in compassion all my diseases you healed
Now I am joyful, free, and at rest
Because of Jesus my Shepherd, My Saviour, and My Friend.

CHAPTER EIGHTEEN: ST MATTHEW

YOUR WORTH

Matthew 16:13-19 (NKJV)

When Jesus came into the region of Caesarea Philippi, He asked His disciples, saying, "Who do men say that I, the Son of Man, am?"

So they said, "Some say John the Baptist, some Elijah, and others Jeremiah or one of the prophets."

He said to them, "But who do you say that I am?"

Simon Peter answered and said, "You are the Christ, the Son of the living God."

Jesus answered and said to him, "Blessed are you, Simon Bar-Jonah, for flesh and blood has not revealed this to you, but My Father who is in heaven. And I also say to you that you are Peter, and on this rock I will build My church, and the gates of Hades shall not prevail against it.

THOUGHT

*O*ne of my favourite musicals is West Side Story. There is a song in it called 'Gee Officer Krupke', where the members of the Jet gang pretend to explain to the officer how societal forces set them on the path to gang life. A judge, a psychiatrist, and a social worker attempt to diagnose the gang members' troubles, but none can get to the root of the matter.

As we go through life, society seeks to put labels on us and pigeon-hole us. It will tell us we have a problem or are a problem, but it cannot cure what truly ails the human heart. All the world can tell us is to conform and not stand out, but some of these labels can be destructive. They can be more like a judgement over us that we are not allowed to escape from.

Jesus is the only one who can tell us who we really are and who can liberate us from all the lies we've been labelled with. When society writes us off, Jesus sets us right with Him.

In the eyes of the Pharisees and the Jewish elites, Peter was just a common fisherman. But in Jesus, he was called an Apostle, a chosen vessel for the Kingdom of God.

When we see Christ for who He is, the Son of the Living God, we will no longer value ourselves according to the scales of the world. We will see our worth through the sacrifice of our Saviour on the cross and know we are a child of a King.

WORD STUDY

Christ
Χριστὸς
In Greek, this is **Christos** which means anointed One; the Messiah, the Christ. From chrio; Anointed One, i.e., The Messiah, an epithet of Jesus

Blessed
Μακάριος
In Greek, this is **Makarios**, which means happy, blessed, to be envied. A prolonged form of the poetical makar; supremely blest; by extension, fortunate, well off

was not revealed
ἀπεκάλυψέν
In Greek, this is **apekalypsen**, which means to uncover, bring to light, reveal. From apo and kalupto; to take off the cover, i.e. disclose

PRAYER

Thank you, Lord Jesus, that you have adopted me as your child. But sometimes, I behave like an orphan and forget who I am, and I put back on the labels of the world. But you have given me new life in Christ and destiny in you. Help me to live my life from my identity in Christ. Let my life be a testimony so others may come to know of the hope that's available in you.

In Jesus' Name, Amen.

POEM

~

In the beloved
Dead to sin Alive in Christ
Everlasting Life
New Creation in Christ
The Head and not the tail
I am God's workmanship
Transformed by the renewing of my mind
Yours forever

CHAPTER NINETEEN: ST MARK

THE WORD WORKS

Mark 4:26-29 (NKJV)

And He said, "The kingdom of God is as if a man should scatter seed on the ground, and should sleep by night and rise by day, and the seed should sprout and grow, he himself does not know how. For the earth yields crops by itself: first the blade, then the head, after that the full grain in the head. But when the grain ripens, immediately he puts in the sickle, because the harvest has come."

THOUGHT

*T*here is something quite miraculous about God's word. For years, I struggled with legalism, perfectionism, and just constantly trying and failing to live for God in my own strength. It was like I had blinders on; I could not figure out how to break free.

When God started to show me how vital His word is, it was life-changing. There is miraculous power in His word and all we have to do is immerse ourselves in it. If we take the time to be in God's word, it will change us.

It is not an immediate transformation, but like the seed in the natural ground, the seed of God's word in the soil of our hearts will take root and as we water it with prayer, we will see it germinate and flourish.

God had to work on a lot of brokenness in me before the seed of His word started to yield fruit. I had a lot of insecurities, fears, pride, and anger. I am amazed when I think back to my teen years and early twenties. I loved God and had wonderful experiences in prayer, but deep down, I was a mess and God knew it.

I felt God calling me when I was in my teens, I'm older now, and I feel I'm just beginning to step into what the Lord requires of me. God is a patient farmer; He knows how to break up our rough places, till the ground, and nurture the seed. If we cooperate with Him, then by faith and patience, we will reap the promised harvest in our lives.

WORD STUDY

[the] stalk,

χόρτον

In Greek, this is **chorton**, which means grass, herbage, growing grain, hay. Apparently a primary word; a 'court' or 'garden', i.e. herbage or vegetation

[the] head,

στάχυν (stachyn)

In Greek, this is **stachyn**, which means a head of grain. From the base of histemi; a head of grain

grain

σῖτον

In Greek, this is **siton**, which means wheat, grain. Also plural irregular neuter sita of uncertain derivation; grain, especially wheat

[that] ripens

πλήρης

In Greek, this is **plērēs**, which means full, abounding in, complete, completely occupied with. From pletho; replete, or covered over; by analogy, complete

PRAYER

Thank you, Lord, for your Word. It is a lamp to my feet and light to my path. Give me a heart, Lord, for your word. Give me understanding when I read it. Help me to apply faith that it is transforming my heart and renewing my mind even when change seems to take longer than I want. Help me to be patient and diligent in studying and meditating on the Bible. Thank you that you are making me more like you and people will see the fruit of the Holy Spirit in my life.

In Jesus' Name, Amen.

POEM

∿

The Word of God is my daily bread
It is living water
It is my source of strength
It is my guiding light for every day,
It is wisdom for every decision I make
The Word of God is eternal life;
I will meditate on it day and night,
And surely goodness and mercy will follow me
All the days of my life.

CHAPTER TWENTY: ST LUKE

COUNT THE COST

Luke 14:27-28 (NKJV)

And whoever does not bear his cross and come after Me cannot be My disciple. For which of you, intending to build a tower, does not sit down first and count the cost, whether he has enough to finish it?

THOUGHT

*W*hat do you do when taking a stand, causing your family to suffer temporarily? Moses took a stand which made Pharaoh afflict God's people the more. Mordecai took a stand which resulted in the Jewish people almost being wiped out.

Obedience has a price tag, and being a disciple of Jesus Christ means persecution is inevitable because our lives will clash with the way the world lives.

Sometimes, we make the decision to not obey God for fear of the repercussions it may have on us or those we care about. I don't take a stand on the anti-Christian curriculum in case my kids get singled out and teased. But what price will they pay if I keep silent?

Playing down my Christian faith to not make my family feel awkward or cause arguments or have to put up with their ridicule and disrespect. But what if I'm the only light for Jesus they ever see?

There is a cost to follow Jesus, but don't let Satan lie to you that not standing up doesn't have a cost as well. It does; what we do and don't do always impacts those around us. Let's encourage and support our fellow brothers and sisters in living confidently for Christ. We are the salt and light of the earth, and if we lose our saltiness, we are no longer effective for the Kingdom of God.

WORD STUDY

disciple
μαθητής
In Greek, this is **mathētēs**, which means a learner, disciple, and
pupil. From manthano; a learner, i.e., Pupil

[and] count
ψηφίζει
In Greek, this is **psēphizei**, which means to reckon, compute,
calculate. From psephos; to use pebbles in enumeration, i.e., to
compute

cost
δαπάνην (dapanēn)
In Greek, this is **dapanēn**, which means cost, expense. From
dapto; expense

he has [the resources]
ἔχει
In Greek, this is **echei**, which means to have, hold, possess.
Including an alternate form, scheo skheh'-o; a primary verb;
to hold

complete [it]?
ἀπαρτισμόν (apartismon)

In Greek, this is **apartismon**, which means completion, perfection. From a derivative of aparti; completion

PRAYER

Heavenly Father, you have shown me that following you will not always be easy. I will be living contrary to the world's way of thinking and believing, so there will be times I will experience rejection, opposition, and persecution. God, I ask that you would strengthen me to be brave and not be afraid. I want to be a person of conviction and integrity. I declare I am strong in the Lord and in the power of your might, as I make a stand for you. I pray someone will see you through me and be drawn to give their lives to you.

In Jesus' Name, Amen.

POEM

Lord, I have heard your call
I leave my past behind and I've counted the cost.
Like a good soldier I fight the fight of faith
I don't live by feelings I walk by faith.
I put on the whole armour of God
Daily I take up my cross
I run my race so I will win
To hear well done
Good and Faithful servant
Enter in

CHAPTER TWENTY-ONE: ST JOHN

JESUS OUR DEFENDER

John 8:10-11 (NKJV)

When Jesus had raised Himself up and saw no one but the woman, He said to her, "Woman, where are those accusers of yours? Has no one condemned you?"

She said, "No one, Lord."

And Jesus said to her, "Neither do I condemn you; go and sin no more."

THOUGHT

*T*his setup by the Pharisees makes Jesus "look like" He's in a no-win situation.

If Jesus had just said "stone her", the Pharisees would have said He was inconsistent. How can He accept publicans and harlots and then turn around and judge this woman?

If He had said "don't stone her", the Pharisees would say Jesus is an enemy to the Law of Moses and that He came to destroy the law and the prophets.

What does Jesus do?

He does not get into a debate about the law or excuse the woman's guilt.

He moves the focus off the woman and onto the accusers.

This is what the Pharisees didn't factor into the equation...**themselves.**

The only one who has the authority to judge us is God. Jesus tells these men, look at the sin in your own life. Jesus measures back to them the same measure they gave to this woman. They exposed her, so Jesus exposes their hearts.

Now, let's look at how Jesus handles the sinful woman.

This is the first time in this whole encounter Jesus speaks to the woman, and He asks her a question,

Woman, where are those accusers of yours?

Jesus wants this woman to see that no one had the authority to cast a stone at her.

What can we learn?

When someone accuses us even if it's valid, if we allow Him, Jesus will deal with our accusers.

Jesus then asked the woman, "...*has no one condemned you?*"

The Pharisees did not have the right to condemn her to death.

What can we learn?

Jesus does not permit other people to judge us.

Jesus is the only one that can cast a stone, but He didn't.

Jesus gives the gift of 'no condemnation', and this empowered the woman to go and sin no more.

Jesus is GRACE FIRST (Neither do I condemn you) and then TRUTH (Go and sin no more).

WORD STUDY

Accusers
κατήγοροί
In Greek, this is **katēgoroi**, which means an accuser,
prosecutor. From kata and agora; against one in the assembly,
i.e., a complainant at law; specially, Satan

Condemned
κατέκρινεν
In Greek, this is **katekrinen**, which means to condemn, judge
worthy of punishment. From kata and krino; to judge against,
i.e., Sentence

PRAYER

Lord Jesus, I thank you that you are my defender. Even when I have done wrong, you do not allow my enemies to destroy me. But you confront my sin with grace and truth. Thank you for your words that give life, conviction, and healing to me. I am undone in your presence, enveloped by your grace, and empowered to go and sin no more. Thank you for the blood of Jesus that washes away my sin. Thank you for your gift of forgiveness. May my heart always be tender to the work of the Holy Spirit. Help me to be quick to repent when you convict me and live in obedience to your will.

In Jesus' Name, Amen.

POEM

~

I was guilty, I was lost, I was broken, and unseen
All my sin and shame constantly tormented me
A prison of my making, unworthy of saving
The weight of accusations;
I deserved the condemnation
I lay waiting for your judgement;
But instead, you spoke words of comfort
Such mercy undeserved
You exchanged my pain
For eternal worth

CHAPTER TWENTY-TWO: ST JOHN

THE ABIDING LIFE

John 15:5 (NKJV)

"I am the vine, you are the branches. He who abides in Me, and I in him, bears much fruit; for without Me you can do nothing.

THOUGHT

*O*bserve any tree, flower, or plant. You never hear it moaning and groaning and straining to grow. It just happens naturally because it's connected to all the right sources it needs—soil, water, nutrients, and sunlight. Being and staying connected makes growth effortless. That's how God wants it to be for us, as natural as our growth is from a babe to an adult. You can't rush the process, it just happens day by day.

For a vine to produce its best fruit, it is immersed in the best environment. It doesn't uproot and replant itself next to a cabbage patch.

Abiding means to immerse ourselves in Christ. Learn His ways, character, and nature. The disciples followed Jesus, observed Jesus, listened to Jesus, asked Jesus questions, and obeyed the instructions of Jesus. Their whole lives were consumed by His, so much so that when Jesus was resurrected and the disciples were empowered to continue His ministry, people around them recognised that they had been with Jesus.

We want people to say the same of us, but that will only happen as we spend time with God.

If what comes out of us is more bitter fruit than sweet, we need to spend more time abiding with the Lord. The only way the fruit of the Holy Spirit will ever grow is if we give it time.

Let's come humbly to Jesus, acknowledging our utter dependence on Him and inability to be like Him unless He changes us. Our prayer must be, *Lord, give me a heart like yours.*

As we choose to abide in Him, His nature will flow through us to others. That's how we change and change people and circumstances around us.

WORD STUDY

vine
ἄμπελος
In Greek, this is **ampelos**, which means a vine, grape-vine.
Probably from the base of amphoteros and that of halon; a vine

branches.
κλήματα
In Greek, this is **klēmata**, which means a branch, shoot, twig.
From klao; a limb or shoot

remains
μένων
In Greek, this is **menōn**, which means to remain, abide, stay,
wait; with acc: I wait for, await. A primary verb; to stay

PRAYER

Dear God, only abiding in you will I become your disciple, only abiding in your word will I know the truth that sets me free. Liberate me from all my limitations, for in you I am free to love and fulfil my destiny.

Lord, grant me the ability to delight in your word and in your ways. Remove all that displeases you and make me Christ-like.

In Jesus' Name, Amen.

POEM

~

There is no other place I'd rather be,
No other place than sitting at your feet,
Like Mary just listening to your words of life,
Healing my heart and renewing my mind
There's no other place I'd rather be
Than in your presence
Lord Jesus

CHAPTER TWENTY-THREE: ST JOHN

SERVING FROM THE SIDELINES

John 19:25 (NKJV)

Now there stood by the cross of Jesus His mother, and His mother's sister, Mary the wife of Clopas, and Mary Magdalene.

THOUGHT

One evening, I was sitting quietly listening to the Bible on my phone, when this verse jumped out to me.

A quick search online led me to verses such as Mark 15: 40-41 and Luke 8:33 revealing that several female disciples followed Jesus, supported Him from their own possessions, and were present around the time of His crucifixion. Suddenly, my imagination was filled with a picture of sisterhood, love, and support.

Sadly, we don't learn much about these women's individual stories. Seven are mentioned by name in the gospels, and we are given a backstory for four of them, (Mary the mother of Jesus,

Mary and Martha sisters to Lazarus and Mary Magdalene). But, for the most-part, women disciples are nameless.

None of these women are centre stage in the gospels with the possible exception of Jesus' mother. However, I think it's beautiful that when these women are mentioned, it's being in close proximity to one another and to their Lord and Saviour.

In the end, isn't that what we want to be said of us?

Each of us, at some point, will be like one of these faithful women to someone else. We are not always centre stage in life, sometimes we are serving from the sidelines. But that calling is no less valid. Can we let go of our ego and be content to be a footnote?

There are many brief appearances and nameless people in the Bible, but each person was crucial to the bigger story unfolding.

Jochebed, Moses Mother.

Anna the prophetess, who saw the baby Jesus and spoke about Him to everyone waiting for God to set Jerusalem free.

The three Magi also known as the wise men.

Ananias who prayed for the Apostle Paul's sight.

To name a few.

These individuals were not the main characters but did their part. To God, that's what matters. We all contribute something important to the Kingdom of God. So, my encouragement to you is be faithful to do your part because it matters. I think if we could interview any of the women who were Jesus' disciples, they would tell us the view from the sidelines was still lifechanging.

WORD STUDY

Near
παρὰ
In Greek, this is **parab**, which means beside, in the presence of;
acc: alongside of

Stood
Είστήκεισαν
In Greek, this is **Heistēkeisa**, which means to stand

PRAYER

Lord Jesus, make me content to play whatever role you give me in the lives of others. Make me your holy vessel, a willing instrument ready for the master's use, to be a voice of encouragement, a smile of assurance, and a hug of comfort. Let me be your hands and feet. Lord Jesus, love others through me and may my life reflect you, so that others will want to know you as their loving Saviour and Lord.

In Jesus' Name, Amen.

POEM

~

Thank you Jesus for making me a part of the Body of Christ.
If I am the hands, let me clap for joy and be a hand of friendship
If I am an eye, let me see all that is good in others
If I am the feet, let me be the feet of peace swift to share the
good news of Jesus
If I am the ear, let me listen well to the hearts of others so I may
be more understanding
If I am a nose, let me smell the beauty of God's creation,
If I am a mouth, let me speak the truth in love and sing God's
praises
If I am an elbow, let me gently nudge my fellow man nearer
to you.
If I am a knee, help me bow before you always in humility.
Whatever I am and all things, I will give God thanks.

CHAPTER TWENTY-FOUR: ROMANS

RPJ

Romans 14:17 (NKJV)

for the kingdom of God is not eating and drinking, but righteousness and peace and joy in the Holy Spirit.

THOUGHT

*R*ighteous + Peace = Joy

These three elements are in this order for a reason. How do we get to righteousness? We have to start with godliness.

Godliness is putting God first in our lives. Anything we put before God is called an idol. I remember I struggled terribly with perfection. I had this running tape in my head that kept saying "what's wrong with me?".

I did not have peace in my soul at all. I wanted to be perfect. I wanted to be right all the time, which was an impossible goal to reach.

The Bible teaches in Romans that only Jesus can gift us righteousness. Only Jesus puts us in right standing with God. Only Jesus can take all that is wrong with us and make us right.

When we are in a relationship with God, He blesses us with His peace. Then He gives us the ability to start living right and when we do that, here comes the joy we always wanted in life.

Getting over that first hurdle is tough. By nature, we want to be our own boss. We don't want God to rule over us. So, we tell ourselves there is no God, so that gets rid of the problem, right???

Wrong!!

As long as people resent God and remain hostile to Him, we will never know true peace and joy. Our lives will always feel like something is missing, and it is.

We were created to be in relationship with God and not to go through life struggling by ourselves.

If you want peace today, reach out to the source of it. Ask Jesus into your heart. It's a decision you will never regret.

WORD STUDY

of righteousness,
δικαιοσύνη

In Greek, this is **dikaiosynē**, which means from dikaios; equity; specially justification

peace,
εἰρήνη

In Greek, this is **eirēnē**, which is probably from a primary verb eiro; peace; by implication, prosperity

joy
χαρὰ

In Greek, this is **chara**, which means joy, gladness, a source of joy. From chairo; cheerfulness, i.e., calm delight

PRAYER

Thank you, Heavenly Father, that it is your good pleasure to give me the Kingdom. Help me to cease striving for things and instead seek your Kingdom and righteousness first. Be Lord over my life in every area and where I struggle to surrender; I bring that struggle to you. I bring you all of me without fear because you know everything about me and you still invite me to draw near to you. Change my heart and mind. I desire your joy and peace but I must also desire your Lordship and will for my life. Thank you, I can trust you with my whole heart.

In Jesus' Name, Amen.

POEM

~

Righteousness springs from faith in Jesus Christ
As I trust in His death, burial, and resurrection
For me He gave His life.
Righteousness and Peace Kiss
And peace flows like a river of Joy
Unspeakable and full of glory
It is sweet, it is Divine
It is sacred
It is Holy
It is joy of the God-kind
It is Spirit-given
His Kingdom within
That transforms me to be more like my King.

CHAPTER TWENTY-FIVE: 1 CORINTHIANS

❦

ANOINTED ADMIN

---

1 Cor. 12:28 (NKJV)

And God has appointed these in the church: first apostles, second prophets, third teachers, after that miracles, then gifts of healings, helps, administrations, varieties of tongues.

THOUGHT

I must have read or heard this verse dozens of times over the years, but this particular morning in my devotional time with the Lord, this word caught my attention.

ADMINISTRATIONS!!

You mean not only is the word administration in the Bible, but it was GOD's IDEA!!! I was shocked.

I have worked in admin for most of my career, not because this was my chosen profession but rather something I fell into. To me, admin was never a job I felt proud of; it never sounded like a valid career. I never like being asked the question, what do you do for a living? It just didn't seem important or interesting.

Admin felt like the job on the sidelines, looking through the window at the people getting to do the real stuff that mattered. (I cringe when I think of my attitude now).

But when I read this scripture, I realised that administration had meaning and value to **God**; it was His idea. Suddenly, all my years of admin work no longer felt like a colossal waste of my life. My work as an administrator could be worship to God.

I wasn't just an administrator; I was an anointed administrator. Now, my prayer became, *"God, show me what an administrator looks like from your perspective, not functioning like the world but bringing God's Kingdom into my everyday work"*.

WORD STUDY

church
ἐκκλησία
In Greek, this is **ekklesia**, which comes from a compound of ek
and a derivative of kaleo; a calling out, i.e. a popular meeting,
especially a religious congregation

has appointed
ἔθετο
In Greek, this is **etheto**, which means to put, place, lay, set, fix,
establish. A prolonged form of a primary theo to place

helping,
ἀντιλήμψεις
In Greek, this is **antilēmpseis**, which means to help,
ministration; one who aids. From antilambanomai; relief

administration,
κυβερνήσεις
In Greek, this is **kybernēseis**, which means (lit: steering,
piloting), governing, government. From kubernao; pilotage

PRAYER

Lord Jesus, thank you. Our work matters to you, and through you, it has value and worth. You have given everyone gifts and abilities as it pleases you for your glory. Help us to see the value in it and not demean it or allow others to in any way. Thank you that you give honour to those things that others may value less. Help us to remember to surrender our work to you and ask you to help and anoint us to do our jobs well. Help us to be grateful and thankful even in the challenging times and less desirable aspects of the role. Help us to do our work as unto you. I pray others will see that difference and even open doors to share Christ with others.

In Jesus' Name, Amen.

POEM

~

All I could see was a lump of clay
Unshapely, unsightly, for that I would not pay
You smiled and said there is beauty here wait and see
I smirked not likely and kissed my teeth.
Gently you begin to press and shape
The dull clay responding to every move you made
Before my eyes, that dull clay began to take shape
What I had despised
You made come alive.
Mesmerised by the work of your hands
I asked why did I not see what this clay could be?
You smiled and replied
Little clay, you only looked at what you were
I look and see your possibilities.

CHAPTER TWENTY-SIX: EPHESIANS

GRACE

Ephesians 2: 8-9 (AMP)

For it is by grace [God's remarkable compassion and favor drawing you to Christ] that you have been saved [actually delivered from judgment and given eternal life] through faith. And this [salvation] is not of yourselves [not through your own effort], but it is the [undeserved, gracious] gift of God; not as a result of [your] works [nor your attempts to keep the Law], so that no one will [be able to] boast or take credit in any way [for his salvation].

THOUGHT

I will NEVER EVER get over grace.

It would baffle me in the early days of my salvation, when I clearly woke up on the wrong side of the bed, not bothering to pray, being grouchy to everyone all day and being thoroughly miserable, I would still sense God's voice in my heart wanting to talk to me.

"Why do you want to talk to me?" I'd say incredulously. *"I'm not being good today. I can't be good all the time,"* I would say with attitude.

I believed for so long, my relationship with God was based on my behaviour and that God was only interested in me when I was "the good girl" and wanted nothing to do with me when I wasn't.

God obviously didn't get the memo.

I battled with low self-worth for many years, and felt and walked around like I was the worst Christian on the planet. Yet, I had experienced the absolute relentless grace of God rescue me when I was furthest away.

Grace, for me, was the constant reminder that God was still there. I could scarcely believe it, that He would want anything to do with me.

But that is the beauty of grace; it is the undeserved gift of God. This verse says our works and attempts to keep the law will never acquire it. God's salvation and His grace can only be humbly received.

WORD STUDY

by grace
χάριτί
In Greek, this is **charity**, which means from chairo;
graciousness, of manner or act

saved
σεσωσμένοι
In Greek, this is **sesōsmeno**, which means to save, heal,
preserve, rescue. From a primary sos; to save, i.e., Deliver or
protect

works
ἔργων
In Greek, this is **ergon**, from a primary ergo; toil; by
implication, an act

PRAYER

Heavenly Father, the grace of God leaves me humbled, face to the floor in complete awe of your love. I am overwhelmed by your goodness and faithfulness towards me. Even when I am unfaithful, broken, or push you away, there you are, still speaking grace over me and calling me your own. I will never get over the wonder of your grace. Thank you for loving me unconditionally.

In Jesus' Name, Amen.

POEM

~

Grace
Goodness of God leading me to repentance
River of love flowing to my heart and soul
Acceptance and assurance in Christ my Saviour
Christ-like nature
Made His child His own

CHAPTER TWENTY-SEVEN:
COLOSSIANS

❧

FINDING MY PLACE

Colossians 1:15-18 (The Message Bible)

We look at this Son and see the God who cannot be seen. We look at this Son and see God's original purpose in everything created. For everything, absolutely everything, above and below, visible and invisible, rank after rank after rank of angels— everything got started in him and finds its purpose in him. He was there before any of it came into existence and holds it all together right up to this moment. And when it comes to the church, he organises and holds it together, like a head does a body.

THOUGHT

*H*ave you ever had one of those days where you think I'm just here taking up space? You question your worth or place in the world. Deep in your soul, there is a desire to know I have a purpose.

This scripture is refreshing, letting us know that *everything* got started in Jesus and finds its place in Him. What does that mean to us? It means there is a source; we have a beginning and a creator that we can look to and know that if Jesus set our lives in motion, it was with a purpose in mind.

To know about ourselves, we have to look at Jesus. When we trust who He says He is, we know God doesn't make mistakes. He created a perfect place for us.

Look around you, everything God created has a function and a purpose, but look again, they also have a perfect place—a place where they work at their optimum and flourish. Everything from the computer I'm typing on, to the flowers in the garden, imagine if I tried to switch them around and wanted the flowers to do the job of the computer and the computer to bloom like a flower...*CRRRAZY* right!! The results would be less than impressive.

Sometimes, we beat up on ourselves and say we're not smart when the truth is, we are just not in the right place.

Okay, Okay you say, but where exactly is that????

Rest assured, God knows exactly where you are and exactly where to place you. If you are struggling, follow God's prescription and cast your care on Him. More often than not, God has been speaking to our hearts, but we're too busy or too scared to listen and trust Him.

Ask Him to help you find your place and ask Him for the strength to make the changes the Holy Spirit leads you to.

Your place may mean a physical move like changing careers, or it may be a change of mind, attitude, or perspective. Whatever it may be, take that step of faith. Remember, no one else can take your place, and YOUR place is waiting just for you.

WORD STUDY

all things
πάντα

In Greek, this is **panta**, which means all, the whole, every kind of. Including all the forms of declension; apparently a primary word; all, any, every, the whole

were created,
ἐκτίσθη

In Greek, this is **ektisthē**, which means to create, form, shape, make, always of God. Probably akin to ktaomai; to fabricate, i.e. Found

hold together
συνέστηκεν

In Greek, this is **synestēken**, which means to place together, commend, prove, exhibit; instrans: I stand with; To be composed of, cohere.

have preeminence.
πρωτεύων

In Greek, this is **prōteuōn**, which means to have preeminence, be chief, be first. From protos; to be first.

PRAYER

Heavenly Father, thank you that when I look to you, I see that I was created for a purpose, that the plans you have for me are good and full of hope. My life is held together by you; the closer I draw to you, the more content I am. Guide and lead me day by day, shape my life to what you would have it be, so my life will always bring you glory.

In Jesus' Name, Amen.

POEM

~

I look to the Son, where all things began.
In your mind, I was perfection
With Holy intention
But in this world, I have been marred
Sin has left its ugly scars
But I cried to the one who is not far
You became my saviour and rescuer
Here I am in your loving hands
You lead me back to your original plan
My life bound together by your Spirit and Word.
My life testifies of your wondrous works.

CHAPTER TWENTY-EIGHT:
COLOSSIANS

❧

LONGSUFFERING PATIENCE

Colossians 3:12 (NKJV)

Therefore, as the elect of God, holy and beloved, put on tender mercies, kindness, humility, meekness, longsuffering;

THOUGHT

*W*e never hear much said about the fruit of longsuffering, but I'm starting to have a strange appreciation for it. There are lessons that we learn over time that are tough to grasp, but when we do, we place great value on the wisdom, knowledge, and insight we now possess.

For some things in life, there are no shortcuts, and we should be thankful about it. Imagine if what took you ten years to learn was squeezed into one year. You can say, OUCH!! I don't know if I would have hung in there past three weeks.

God takes His time with us, not because He is slow but because He cares. Certain skill sets are dying out because they require patience to achieve exquisite craftsmanship. Nowadays, the quicker you can make and create, the better. Never mind about longevity, we live in the disposable generation.

Jesus is not like that; He is never in a hurry to do anything. God does not show us all our faults that need fixing at one time, but like the wise master builder He is, He takes His time dismantling the old erroneous belief systems in us and building the new ones.

Our lives are the house built on the rock that is Jesus.

I like to think of longsuffering as patience stretched out with a rolling pin. We endure unfavourable circumstances with a good attitude. We grow our capacity to tolerate delay and problems or suffering. It is not an easy fruit to grow up into, but God is longsuffering in His kindness to help us learn it.

WORD STUDY

clothe yourselves with
Ἐνδύσασθε

In Greek, this is **Endysasthe**, which means to put on, clothe (another). From en and duno; to invest with clothing

[and] patience
μακροθυμίαν

In Greek, this is **makrothymian**, which means patience, forbearance, longsuffering. From the same as makrothumos; longanimity, i.e., forbearance or fortitude.

PRAYER

Dear God, being patient does not always come easy for me, and I live in a world that does not always celebrate longsuffering. Life is always in a rush.

Teach me, Lord, to grow the fruit of patience. Lord, I admit I have shied away from pursuing patience and the fruit of longsuffering. But through you, I see this muscle needs to be developed if I am going to fight the good fight of faith, finish the race, and keep the faith.

I trust you, Lord, to develop my character so that I will not lack in the area of my Christian faith.

Thank you, Lord. In Jesus' Name I pray.

Amen.

POEM

~

I am patience
I am excellence personified
I am in no hurry to make sure everything is just right.
I delight in my work to make you all you are meant to be;
I may take my time,
But when I'm finished, you will be a thing of beauty
Do not worry nor fret
Trust me
And every area of your life I will perfect;
You will be complete lacking nothing,
By faith and patience you'll obtain the promise.
I am born out of adversity, from the testing of your faith
If you let me, I will teach you how to bend but not to break.
I am patience
A unique fruit
You'll find me rich in goodness
Just taste and see.

CHAPTER TWENTY-NINE: HEBREWS

WE ARE HIS JOY

Hebrews 12:2 (NLT)

We do this by keeping our eyes on Jesus, the champion who initiates and perfects our faith. Because of the joy awaiting him, he endured the cross, disregarding its shame. Now he is seated in the place of honour beside God's throne.

THOUGHT

To gain the life we want, give up what we have...WHAT!!!

It's like the old story of the little girl who held a pearl so tight in her hand. Her father asked her to let go of it so that he could give her something in its place, but she refused. Little did she know her father had a **string of pearls** to give her in place of the **one.**

It's an easier trade to make when you know the payoff.

And the end of a thing can seem more appealing than the journey to get there.

So, how do we stay focused?

Remind yourself why you wanted to achieve your goal in the first place. Picture yourself in that place of success. See the end result far outweighing the sacrifices you have to make. Then break your goals down into manageable achievable steps and take it one day at a time.

Hebrews 12:2 says, '*...for the **joy** set before Jesus He endured the cross, despising the shame...*'

Do you know, **you** and **I** were the joy Jesus had on His mind when He went to the cross? He endured the pain so that everybody could have a relationship with Him.

Make up in your mind today to endure the tough times to achieve your goals.

Fix your sight on Jesus, follow His example, and remember the joy is greater than the struggle.

WORD STUDY

Let us fix our eyes
ἀφορῶντες

In Greek, this is **aphorōntes**, which means to look away from (something else) to, see distinctly. From apo and horao; to consider attentively

pioneer
ἀρχηγὸν

In Greek, this is **archēgon**, which means originator, author, founder, prince, leader. From arche and ago; a chief leader

perfecter
τελειωτὴν

In Greek, this is **teleiōtēn**, which means a perfecter, completer, finisher. From teleioo; a completer, i.e., Consummater

joy
χαρᾶς

In Greek, this is **charas**, which means joy, gladness, a source of joy. From chairo; cheerfulness, i.e., Calm delight

endured
ὑπέμεινεν

In Greek, this is **hypemeinen**, which means from hupo and

meno; to stay under, i.e., Remain; figuratively, to undergo, i.e., Bear, have fortitude, persevere

PRAYER

Thank you, Lord Jesus, that you thought of me when you were dying for my sins on the cross. The thought of me brought you joy. God, your word says the joy of the Lord is my strength. Help me to draw on your joy to keep moving forward. Even in tough times, help me keep my eyes on you and allow you to perfect my faith. Help me to run my race well that one day, I will hear you say to me, "Well done, my good and faithful servant".

In Jesus' Name, Amen.

POEM

God, you are my example of faith,
Of endurance and how to run my race,
To press through all the pain and shame,
To press past all the distractions and games,
Lord, help me to hold to the truth
Keep my eyes on the true prize
That is you;
Pursue the upward call of God, in Jesus Christ
Make my election sure
Stay focused on Christ.

CHAPTER THIRTY: ST JAMES

OVERCOMING TEMPTATION

James 1:17 (NKJV)

Every good gift and every perfect gift is from above, and comes down from the Father of lights, with whom there is no variation or shadow of turning.

THOUGHT

*V*erse 17 is in the middle of a chapter that starts off encouraging believers to ask for God's wisdom when we are facing tough times.

This verse is set in contrast to what temptation produces, which is sin and death. The Book of James makes it clear that God is not the author of both outcomes. Evil desires lead to sin, which leads to death. God's gifts are good and godly, leading to life.

James seems to highlight a problem some people were having during the trying of their faith. They were misinterpreting their challenging experiences as a temptation from God.

James is encouraging the believers that they are to endure the time of temptation, and they are able to if they depend on God.

Instead, what seemed to be happening was people were giving in to their flesh and blaming God.

James responds swiftly to correct this erroneous belief system by explaining to the believers that it is impossible for God to tempt anyone.

This right here is a teachable moment, how to discern the origin of something in our lives.

Temptation originates from within us, from our own evil desires, and ultimately will produce death.

God's gift, by contrast, comes from above, originating from our Father in Heaven, and produces life.

God is the giver of all that is good because that is His nature. James gives us a revelation of the essence of God that He is so much light in His essence that He doesn't even cast a shadow.

A shadow is an imperfect outline of the real object, and there is no imperfection in God.

Everything about God is light; it is impossible for any darkness to be in Him. Therefore, no gift from God will ever have any evil intention attached to it.

James encourages believers to go back to the Word of God and put their faith in it as the only remedy to save them.

However, James warns the believer that handling the Word of God superficially will not bring about true change in a person's life.

James says just reading the Bible is not enough, we have to study it, meditate on it, and most importantly, put it to work in our daily lives. There must be corresponding actions; otherwise, our Christian life will remain ineffective, and we will only find ourselves caught up in the same cycle of falling into temptation and wondering why we see very little of the maturity of Christ in our lives.

WORD STUDY

Good
δόσις

In Greek, this is **dosis**, which means a giving, gift, donation. From the base of didomi; a giving; by implication, a gift

Perfect
τέλειον

In Greek, this is **teleion**, which means from telos; complete; neuter completeness

Gift
δώρημα

In Greek, this is **dōrēma**, which means a gift, bounty. From doreomai; a bestowment

Of the heavenly lights
φώτων

In Greek, this is **photon**, which means light, a source of light, radiance. From an obsolete phao; luminousness

PRAYER

Lord Jesus, thank you that you do not leave us in any confusion as to the source of our temptation. But you also give us the answer on how to overcome. You draw us back to the Word of God and put it into action. It is a continual daily process. Lord, help me to continue in the Word. Teach me how to study it, and open my heart and mind to believe and understand it. Show me throughout my day on how to put it in practice. Father, as you help me do my part, I trust you to do yours and cause the fruit of Christ to be seen in my life.

In Jesus' Name, Amen.

POEM

~

Lord, you know my every way
How I fuss and fight and stray.
But Lord, you know my heart
I long for peace and calm

The battle in my soul
Only you can conquer all.
I know your will is best.
Yet, surrender is sometimes
A fight to the death.

I must crucify my flesh
Be led by the Spirit
If I want a life that's blessed

So, help me Lord I pray
To obey and let you lead the way
For only in following you
Will I know freedom
And a life that's full.

CHAPTER THIRTY-ONE: JAMES

HEART ISSUES

James 4:1 (AMPC) What leads to strife (discord and feuds) and how do conflicts (quarrels and fightings) originate among you? Do they not arise from you sensual desires that are ever warring in your bodily members?

You are jealous and covet [what others have] and your desires go unfulfilled; [so] you become murderers. [To hate is to murder as far as your hearts are concerned.] You burn with envy and anger and are not able to obtain [the gratification, the contentment, and the happiness that you seek], so you fight and war. You do no have, because you do not ask.

THOUGHT

I really encourage you to read the first four verses, it makes for shocking reading.

The phrases and thoughts that stood out for me were the ones that describe, living out your life trying to obtain contentment and happiness but being unable to obtain it. Imagine never achieving what you are striving for.

Can you think of anything more frustrating???

When I read it, it was like God was telling me the exact state of my heart. I was embarrassed. I'm not saying I was the poster child of James 4: 1-4. But God was drawing my attention to the unease in my heart and His solution for it.

I was embarrassed and repentant because I realised my heart had been this way for too long. But I was grateful and ready for God's remedy which blew me away.

Verse 5- 6

Or do you suppose that the Scripture is speaking to no purpose that says, The Spirit Whom He has caused to dwell in us yearns over us and He yearns for the Spirit [to be welcome] with a jealous love?

But He gives us more and more grace (power of the Holy Spirit, to meet this evil tendency and all others fully). That is why He says, God sets Himself against the proud and haughty, but gives grace [continually] to the lowly (those who are humble enough to receive it).

There it was, just as I was feeling overwhelmed with hopelessness, here was Jesus the God of all hope saying. I already knew what your heart would need and I made provision for it. This scripture has become my daily prayer along with others.

The Spirit of Christ is the only power that can deal with my sinful nature, and if I don't come to Jesus and ask Him to help me. The only thing I'm guaranteed is defeat.

Now my prayer is...

Lord help me to yearn for you as the Holy Spirit yearns for me. I welcome Him and His miraculous power to help me. Lord you already know what I will have to face today and you know my failures and weaknesses. Spirit of grace, help me to be humble and see my need for you and ask for your grace to overcome every evil tendency, that you lovingly provide. Amen.

Verse 8

*Come close to God and He will come close to you. [Recognize that you are] sinners, get your soiled hands clean; [realize that you have been disloyal] wavering individuals with **divided interests**, and purify your hearts [of your spiritual adultery].*

Verse 10

*Humble yourselves [feeling very **insignificant**] in the presence of the Lord, and He will exalt you [He will lift you up and make your lives significant].*

When we are aware of our failures, it can make us want to run and hide out of shame and fear. God is holy in calling us out on our sins but He is not rejecting us, rather He promises that if we come close to Him, He will come close to us. There is no need to fear His anger or punishment because Jesus took all our punishment on the cross. Now we have the promise of God's acceptance that when we come, truly repentant of our sins, He will cleanse us and help us to live the way that pleases Him.

The words 'insignificant 'and 'divided interests' in verses 8 and 10, really stood out for me. Everyone wants to feel significant, that when its all said and done our life will have mattered. God promises to give our life significance. The enemy wants us to feel insignificant and twists our insecurities to find toxic ways to make ourselves feel significant. God made us for a purpose and only He can give our lives true meaning.

Divided interests can mean so many things to every heart. Our hearts can be prone to wonder from the Lord for all sorts of reasons. Distractions don't necessarily have to be sinful, sometimes life just gets super busy and before we know it, we haven't taken the time to invest in our relationship with the Lord. We had divided interests, our focus was on other things.

There are many scriptures that talk about having a "whole heart". I heard a teaching on Jeremiah 29:13 about seeking God with our whole heart. I went through a season where this phrase kept coming to my attention. Whole heart, all my heart, it just kept resonating with me. Then I heard someone give a short teaching on the heart, they encouraged people to ask Jesus to deliver us from division and distraction and knit our hearts together. To pray and ask God to make our hearts whole so we can seek God wholeheartedly. I began to pray this way almost daily, using scriptures like Jeremiah 29:13. We can ask God to help us keep our hearts sensitive to Him. He didn't save us and then leave us to do this Christian thing in our own ability. We are to call on Jesus, He wants us to lean on Him and know He will never let us down. His grace is always available and it is always sufficient for our every need, it is well timed and it will come just when we need it.

WORD STUDY

conflicts

πόλεμοι

In Greek, this is **polemoi** which means a war, battle, strife.
From pelomai; warfare.

Quarrels

μάχαι

In Greek, this is **machai** which means from machomai; a battle,
i.e. controversy.

Passions

ἡδονῶν

In Greek, this is **hēdonōn** which means from handano; sensual
delight; by implication, desire.

at war

στρατευομένων

In Greek, this is **strateuomenōn** which means wage war, fight,
serve as a soldier; fig: of the warring lusts against the soul.

PRAYER

Lord help me to long for you as the Holy Spirit longs for me. I welcome Holy Spirit and His miraculous power into my life to help me. Lord you already know what I will have to face today and you know my failures and weaknesses. Spirit of grace help me to be humble and see my need for you and ask for your grace to empower me to overcome every evil tendency, by the miraculous power that you lovingly provide.

Amen.

POEM

～

My heart filled with torment and lies
Made brittle by quarrels and strife
Grappling for the life I desired
Ending in frustration and thoughts of suicide
Exhausted and weary I cried for help
You didn't waste a moment
You were right there
As I ran to your throne of grace
Your mercy washed away all my pain
Your grace you poured into my soul
Dispelled all the darkness and made me whole.
It was you all along I needed
In the light of your beauty all other strivings ceased
Now each day I run to your throne of grace
Knowing its in you I live and I'm sustained
Failures and weaknesses no longer push me away
You have made provision for me to overcome
By your spirit of grace

CHAPTER THIRTY-TWO: REVELATION

NEW HEAVEN AND NEW EARTH

Revelation 21:1 (NKJV)

Now I saw a new heaven and a new earth, for the first heaven and the first earth had passed away. Also there was no more sea.

THOUGHT

*R*ight at the start, we met the Creator of the universe who made the Heavens and the Earth. Here at the end of time. We see a new Heaven and a new Earth, for the first heaven and the first earth has passed away. God's story has been from the start that His Heavens and His Earth will exist as He intended and that He would dwell with mankind.

Our Creator is an incredible Lord and Saviour.

God has showered us with His love and grace.

He has loved us with an everlasting love. He is in love with you, and He is in love with me. We belong to Him, and He is committed to us. Through His Word, He has spoken truth and promises over us, redeemed, healed, and restored us. He rebuilt us and re-orientated our lives to line up with the Master's purpose.

I encourage you to read the Word of God, study it, and meditate on it. BELIEVE IT.

It's God's love letter to humanity.

It's God talking to YOU through the Bible.

Why don't you open it and see wha God has to say?

I pray you will meet Him in the pages of scripture

And discover

Treasures from God's heart.

WORD STUDY

a new

καινὸν

In Greek, this is **kainon**, which means fresh, new, unused,
novel. Of uncertain affinity; new

heaven

οὐρανὸν

In Greek, this is **ouranon**, which means perhaps from the same
as oros; the sky; by extension, heaven; by implication,
happiness, power, eternity; specially, the Gospel

earth,

γῆν

In Greek, this is **gēn**, which means contracted from a primary
word; soil; by extension a region, or the solid part or the whole
of the terrene globe.

PRAYER

Dear Heavenly Father, help me to do my part to make my election sure. I desire to live with you forever and dwell in the new heaven and new earth where the righteous dwell. Lord, help me to be found faithful; help me to live my life for you. Help me to love you with my heart, soul, mind, and strength. I will also love my neighbour as myself. Teach me to walk in love and grow in the fruit of the Holy Spirit. Make me more like you and give me a passion for the Word of God. Thank you, God, that you came for one such as me. Anoint me to lead others to you.

In Jesus' Name, Amen.

POEM

~

There is a city whose builder and maker is God
Where there is no need for sun, moon, or stars
A place lit by the glory of God
Illuminated by the Lamb.
Where God wipes away tears from every eye
There is no more death, no more sorrow, no more crying
There will all behold Him
Cast our crowns before Him
Worship Him an Adore Him
With ceaseless joy
Our names written in the Lamb's Book of Life

THANK YOU READER

For Being On This Journey With Me.

HOW TO HAVE A PERSONAL RELATIONSHIP WITH THE LORD JESUS

If you don't know Jesus Christ as your Lord and Saviour it would be an honour to introduce you to Him. God is good, He loves you, He cares about you and if you let Him into your heart today, I promise your life will never be the same. The Bible says God knows the thoughts and plans He has for you, to give you a hope and a future. And that journey begins when you accept God as your Lord and Saviour into your life.

In the book of Romans 10:8-13 The Passion Translation

8"God's living message is very close to you, as close as your own heart beating in your chest and as near as the tongue in your mouth."

9 And what is God's "living message"? It is the revelation of faith for salvation, which is the message that we preach. For if you publicly declare with your mouth that Jesus is Lord and believe in your heart that God raised him from the dead, you will experience salvation.

10The heart that believes in him receives the gift of the righteousness of God—and then the mouth gives thanks[c] to salvation.

11 For the Scriptures encourage us with these words:

"Everyone who believes in him will never be disappointed."[d]

Friend, if you are ready to give your life to God, pray this prayer.

Dear Lord Jesus,

I have lived my life without you and I want that to change today. I ask you to forgive me of my sins.

I acknowledge that you died on the cross for me. I believe in my heart and confess with my mouth Jesus Christ is Lord and rose from the dead. I surrender my life to you and ask you Jesus to be my Lord and Saviour.

I receive your gift of salvation. Fill me with your Holy Spirit and empower me to live by faith in you every day.

Thank you.

In Jesus' Name,

Amen.

Precious reader, if you prayed this prayer welcome to the family of God. The Bible says the angels in Heaven rejoice when one sinner repents.

It's important that you find a bible-based church, read the Bible daily, pray, and get connected with other Christians so you grow in your new faith.

If you have made the decision to be a follower of Jesus, I would love to connect with you.

Visit my Contact page on my website www. jeanettemccarthy.com

May God richly bless your life.

NOTES

ABOUT THE AUTHOR

JEANETTE MCCARTHY

Jeanette McCarthy is a freelance writer. This is her second publication. Her first publication, 'God, Me, and Poetry' is available on Amazon.
Her desire is for God to use her writing to encourage, heal, and strengthen others in their journey with the Lord.
www.Jeanette.McCarthy.com
Facebook.com/jeanettefreelancewriter
Twitter.com/jeanettewriter
Instagram.com/jeanettewriter
LinkedIn.com/jeanette-mccarthy-8557923b

MORE BY JEANETTE MCCARTHY

God, Me, and Poetry

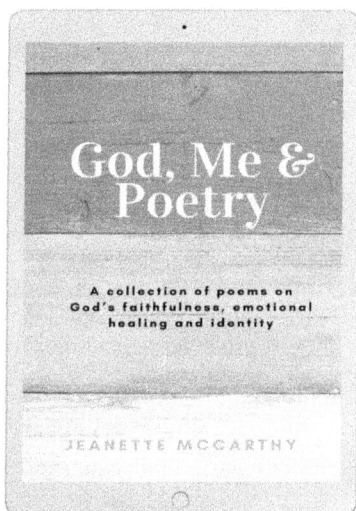

In this book Jeanette shares

a collection of poems on emotional healing,

God's faithfulness and identity.

Her poetry reflects her experiences with

God in her journey of faith.

Poems for Special Occasions Free eBook

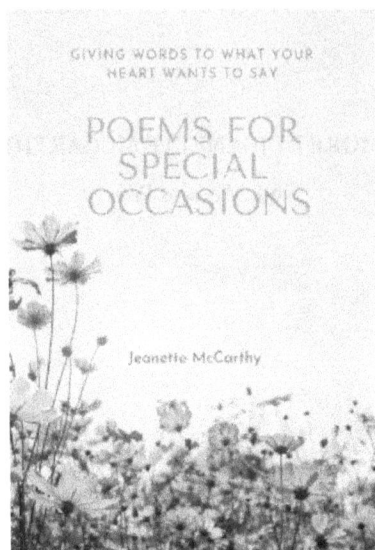

*Free **ebook** of*

poems for special occasions:

Giving words to what

your heart wants to say.

Available on my website:

www.JeanetteMcCarthy.com.

God, Me, and Poetry Podcast

Join me for inspiring poems,
Reflections and conversations.

On Apple, Podcast, Spotify and
other Podcast Platforms

All That Glitters Isn't God

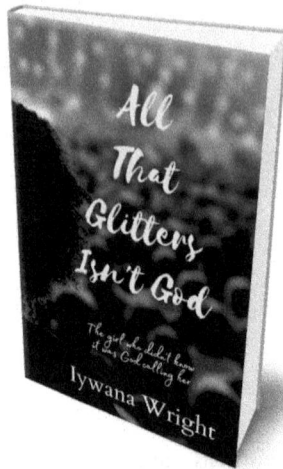

Brace yourself for an emotional summer adventure

Samantha is an eleven girl who didn't know

God was calling her.

Available on Amazon and Kindle.

Jeanette McCarthy

The Helpful VA

Why hire a Virtual Assistant?

As a business owner your time is valuable. I provide the professional admin support your business needs. Saving you time and money, by only paying for hours worked.

SERVICES

Call Clients

Proofreading

Internet Research

Schedule Meetings

Create Word documents

Email Management

Business YouTube Videos

Publishing People of Influence onto

Platforms for Impact.

The Lord gives the word [of power];

the women who bear and publish [the news]

are a great host.

Psalm 68:11 AMPC

www.DivineFlowPublishing.com

CHARITY CLOSE TO MY HEART

Compassion UK

Compassion is a leading children's charity. At our heart is a relentless passion to act on our compassion and empower every child left vulnerable by poverty. Our approach to fighting poverty is highly focused and personal. It's summed up in three simple words: Compassion for children. For 68 years, we've been giving children the opportunity to escape the suffering and fear poverty brings.

We're right with you in believing every child matters. As these famous quotes about children show, kids deserve to be safe, fed, educated and empowered.

Compassionuk.org